COOL ADVENTURE CAREERS

TEST PILOT

By Geoffrey M. Horn

Reading Consultant: Susan Nations, M.Ed.,
author/literacy coach/consultant in literacy development

Gareth Stevens
Publishing

Please visit our web site at **www.garethstevens.com**.
For a free catalog describing Gareth Stevens Publishing's list of high-quality books, call 1-800-542-2595 (USA) or 1-800-387-3178 (Canada).
Gareth Stevens Publishing's fax: 1-877-542-2596

Library of Congress Cataloging-in-Publication Data

Horn, Geoffrey M.
   Test pilot / Geoffrey M. Horn.
       p. cm.—(Cool careers—adventure careers)
       Includes bibliographical references and index.
       ISBN-10: 0-8368-8884-7   ISBN-13: 978-0-8368-8884-3 (lib. bdg.)
       ISBN-10: 0-8368-8891-X   ISBN-13: 978-0-8368-8891-1 (softcover)
       1. Test pilots—Vocational guidance—Juvenile literature. 2. Airplanes—Flight testing—Juvenile literature.   I. Title.
   TL671.7.H66   2007
   629.13023—dc22   2007027666

This edition first published in 2008 by
Gareth Stevens Publishing
A Weekly Reader® Company
1 Reader's Digest Rd.
Pleasantville, NY 10570-7000 USA

Copyright © 2008 by Gareth Stevens, Inc.

Senior Managing Editor: Lisa M. Guidone
Managing Editor: Valerie J. Weber
Creative Director: Lisa Donovan
Designer: Paula Jo Smith
Cover Photo Researcher: Kimberly Babbitt
Interior Photo Researcher: Susan Anderson

Picture credits: Cover, title page © U.S. Air Force/Senior Master Sgt. Thomas Meneguin, sky background: Shutterstock; p. 5 Time & Life Pictures/Getty Images; p. 6 © George Hall/Corbis; p. 8 © Blue Lantern Studio/Corbis; pp. 10, 11 © Bettmann/Corbis; p. 12 © Underwood & Underwood/Corbis; p. 13 NASA; p. 14 Chuck Bigger/AP; pp. 16–17 1st Lt. Cris L'Esperance/U.S. Air Force; pp. 18–19; © Jim Sugar/Corbis; pp. 20–21 NASA; pp. 22–23 Arno Balzarini/AP; p. 24 Sue Ogrocki/AP; p. 26 Boeing; pp. 28–29 NASA

Printed in the United States of America

CPSIA Compliance Information: Batch # 90028101: For further information contact Gareth Stevens, New York, New York at 1-800-542-2595

CONTENTS

Words in the glossary appear in **bold** type the first time they are used in the text.

CHAPTER 1

THE RIGHT STUFF

Most pilots fly planes that have already flown many hundreds of hours. These aircraft carry passengers and **cargo.** Pilots and mechanics need to make sure these planes are totally safe before they take off.

Test pilots are different. They fly planes that are new or changed in some way. Their job is to make sure the planes are safe to fly. A new design can be risky. Today's test pilots try not to take foolish chances. But they know that risk is part of their job.

Going to Extremes

One of the best movies ever made about test pilots is called *The Right Stuff.* (If you haven't seen it, you should.) The film shows the American space program in the 1950s and 1960s. Then, as now, many **astronauts** started out as Air Force or Navy pilots. They learned to fly their aircraft at extreme speeds and heights. They needed the "right stuff" to fly faster, higher, and farther than anyone had flown before.

The early parts of the movie take place at Edwards Air Force Base in California. In those days, being a test pilot was very dangerous. Many pilots lost their lives

The F-22 Raptor needed years of testing before it began flying regular missions for the U.S. Air Force.

testing problem planes. Others crashed while pushing good planes beyond their limits.

Edwards Air Force Base is named for one of those pilots — Glen Edwards. His last job was to test-fly the Northrop YB-49. The jet-powered bomber was fast but hard to control. In his diary Edwards wrote, "Darndest airplane I ever tried to do anything with." He and four other crew members died when their YB-49 crashed on June 5, 1948.

Safety First

A test pilot's job today is much safer than it was sixty years ago. Computers now design and test new aircraft. Before a new plane leaves the ground, a test pilot spends many hours learning how to fly it. Much of this training is done in a **computer simulator.**

The simulator is a working model of the **cockpit.** (The cockpit is the area at the front of the aircraft where the pilot controls the plane.) The simulator's controls look and feel just like the real thing. When a pilot makes a mistake in a simulator, the plane may "crash" — but no one gets hurt.

How Does a Jumbo Jet Get Off the Ground?

A fully loaded jumbo jet can weigh 500 tons (450 metric tons) or more. So how does something so big and heavy get off the runway?

A jet engine is a very powerful machine. But in one way, it works like a household fan. A fan takes in slow-moving air and pushes out fast-moving air. A jet engine takes in air and blasts out hot gases with tremendous force. As these gases shoot from the back of the engine, the plane moves forward. The forward motion is called thrust. The more powerful the engine is, the greater the thrust.

As the plane speeds forward, air flows over and under the wings. The push of air against the wings is called air pressure. As the plane moves, the air pressure under the wings is greater than the air pressure above them. This produces a force called lift. Lift is what pushes the aircraft upward, allowing it to take off.

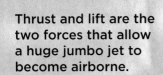

Thrust and lift are the two forces that allow a huge jumbo jet to become airborne.

CHAPTER 2
PUSHING THE ENVELOPE

Have you ever wished you could soar like a bird? An old Greek myth tells of a boy who did just that. The boy's name was Icarus. His father took feathers from birds and wove them into wings. The

wings were held together with wax. The father warned his son that if he flew too high, his wings would fail.

Icarus put on the wings and began to fly. At first, the flight went well. But Icarus wanted to see how high he could go. The ancient writers tell us that he flew too close to the Sun. The wax melted, and his wings fell apart. He plunged into the sea and drowned.

Many of the early test pilots were like Icarus. They wanted to "push the envelope" — to test the limits of their aircraft. They flew and flew until their equipment failed. Sometimes, like Icarus, they came to a sad end.

Early Flights

The airplane era began just over a hundred years ago. Wilbur and Orville Wright made their first powered flight on December 17, 1903. They actually flew four times that day. Their first flight lasted twelve seconds and went 120 feet (37 meters). Their last and longest flight lasted fifty-nine seconds and covered 852 feet (260 m). They made history — even though their best distance was no longer than a few city blocks!

Like the mythical Icarus (right), many test pilots have experienced the thrill of flight — and its dangers.

Wilbur Wright watched his brother Orville pilot the plane that made history at Kitty Hawk, North Carolina, on December 17, 1903.

The Wright Brothers set out to prove that planes could do more — much more. So did rival inventors and pilots. One of those pilots was Eugene Ely. On November 14, 1910, he became the first pilot to take off from a ship. Two months later, he did something even more difficult. On January 18, 1911, he took off from shore and landed his plane on the deck of a ship. The whole history of U.S. Navy planes and **aircraft carriers** starts with his work.

Ely didn't fly much longer. He died when his plane crashed at an air show on October 19, 1911.

Amelia Earhart

Born in Kansas in 1897, Amelia Earhart took her first flight when she was twenty-three. "As soon as I left the ground," she wrote, "I knew I myself had to fly." She started taking flying lessons in January 1921. She learned quickly. In 1922, she flew her small Kinner Airster to a height of 14,000 feet (4,267 m) — a new record for a woman.

Earhart was the first woman to fly the Pitcairn PCA-2. This unusual plane looked a little like a helicopter. It had a propeller in front and spinning blades on top. In April 1931, she flew the PCA-2 to a height of 18,415 feet (5,613 m). This was a new record for any pilot, male or female.

In May 1932, she became the first woman to fly solo across the Atlantic Ocean. Five years later, she took off on a round-the-world trip in a Lockheed L-10 Electra. There was one other crew member — Fred Noonan. They disappeared over the Pacific Ocean in July 1937. They were never heard from again.

Amelia Earhart's achievements as a test pilot made her one of the most famous Americans of the 1930s.

Jackie Cochran set speed records in her Seversky aircraft in the late 1930s.

Test Pilot Pioneers

Not all stories about test pilots end in tragedy. One of the greatest test pilots ever was Jackie Cochran. She flew for about forty years. Cochran set more speed and **altitude** records than anyone else. During **World War II** (1939 to 1945), she led the Women's Air Force Service Pilots (WASP). After the war, she was the first woman to fly faster than the speed of sound.

"Jackie would never give up," said her good friend Chuck Yeager. "She kept right on flying fast planes." She continued to fly until a heart problem forced her to slow down.

Women in Space

Jackie Cochran belonged to a group of thirteen women who tried to become astronauts in the late 1950s. All of them were first-rate pilots. They passed their physical tests in 1960 and 1961. A Russian woman flew in space in 1963. But by then, the program for U.S. women had been canceled. The men who ran the program didn't think women should be astronauts.

Astronaut training for women resumed many years later. In 1983, Sally Ride became the first American woman in space.

Sally Ride — the first American woman in space — flew two *Challenger* space shuttle missions, in 1983 and 1984.

Chuck Yeager piloted an old-time P-51 Mustang fighter plane at a 1998 ceremony honoring World War II pilots.

Yeager was also a great test pilot. He learned how to fly in 1942 while serving with the U.S. Army Air Force. (The Air Force was part of the U.S. Army until 1947.) He flew in combat against the Germans in World War II. After the war, he was chosen to test the Bell X-1 rocket plane.

Nothing could slow him down — not even two broken ribs. He hurt himself badly in a horseback-riding accident in 1947. But two days later, on October 14, he flew his X-1 faster than the speed of sound. He was the first pilot to break the sound barrier. And Yeager kept right on pushing the envelope. On December 12, 1953, he flew an X-1A at 1,650 miles (2,655 kilometers) per hour. That was more than twice the speed of sound — and faster than anyone had flown before.

What Is the Sound Barrier?

Have you ever heard the roar of a jet engine? It's one of loudest sounds around. The noise moves through the air in waves. These sound waves are a bit like waves in water. Scientists have measured the speed of sound under different conditions. At sea level in normal weather, sound waves move through the air at about 770 miles (1,240 km) per hour.

Strange things happen when an aircraft gets close to the speed of sound. The plane moves faster and faster, but the sound waves don't. The sound waves are pushed so hard they bump against each other. The plane may start to vibrate and become very hard to control. Test pilots in the 1940s called this "breaking the sound barrier." Today's aircraft designs make breaking the sound barrier much less scary.

When sound waves are pushed together hard, they form shock waves. The most powerful shock waves form at the tip and tail of the plane. These shock waves are the main cause of the loud noise known as a **sonic boom.** People on the ground hear this booming noise when a plane flies at **supersonic** speeds.

CHAPTER 3

EARNING YOUR WINGS

Many test pilots get their training in the armed forces. The U.S. Air Force has its Test Pilot School at Edwards Air Force Base. The U.S. Naval Test Pilot School is at Patuxent River, Maryland.

Standards at these schools are high. For example, to enter the Air Force Test Pilot School, you need a college degree in math, science, or engineering. You also need many hours of Air Force flying experience. Your body must be

Many top American test pilots get their training in the U.S. Air Force.

in top condition. Poor vision or poor hearing will keep you from being a test pilot. So will frequent dizziness, asthma, or other breathing problems.

Hitting the Books

To become a test pilot, you'll need to spend time in the classroom as well as the cockpit. Today's test pilots must learn all about the planes they fly. At the Naval

Test Pilot School, students have to write reports up to seventy pages long. The toughest thing about the school is "the sheer volume of work," says one student.

Before they grab a joystick, pilots learn the right way to test an aircraft. They also learn how to check test results and report what they find out. Test pilots work closely with aircraft designers. The aircraft makers use the test results to make changes in their designs. Pilots and designers share the same goal — to make the aircraft fly better and more safely.

NASA astronauts experience the ups and downs of weightlessness in their "vomit comet" training sessions.

Riding the "Vomit Comet"

To earn your wings, you need to learn the right stuff in the classroom. Your body needs to have the right stuff, too. Do you have what it takes to be a top test pilot?

One way to find out is to take a ride on the "vomit comet." Riding this plane is a little like riding a roller coaster, only much tougher. When the plane makes a

Foreign Schools and Students

Some foreign students get their test pilot training in the United States. Others train at schools in Canada, Britain, and France. Russia, India, Japan, and Brazil also have test pilot training programs.

The world's first school for military test pilots was founded in Britain in 1943. Today it is known as the Empire Test Pilots' School. The school is located in southern England at Boscombe Down. It trains students from all over the world.

steep climb, your body feels very heavy. At the top of the climb, just before the aircraft starts downward, you feel as if you weigh nothing at all. This plane is used to train NASA astronauts. (NASA — the National Aeronautics and Space Administration — runs the U.S. space program.) Why is it nicknamed the "vomit comet"? The weightless feeling makes many first-time riders throw up.

Here's another tough test — the "fuge." (*Fuge* is short for *centrifuge*.) The fuge looks like an amusement-park ride — but riding in it isn't much fun. You sit inside a capsule that looks and feels like an airplane cockpit. A long arm connects the capsule to the base. As the base spins, the arm and capsule speed up. As you move faster and faster, you feel as if a tremendous force is pressing on your chest. Your heart pumps harder. Your vision gets weaker. You feel dizzy. If you're not careful, you may black out.

Pilots wear special suits to deal with this force. They also learn other ways to handle the stress. Pilots need to keep their minds clear and sharp at all times if they want to keep control of their aircraft.

Introduced in the 1960s, the SR-71 Blackbird flew at more than three times the speed of sound. It could reach a height of 85,000 feet (25,900 m) above sea level.

Test Pilot Speed Records

On July 28, 1976, Air Force Captain Eldon W. Joersz flew 2,193 miles (3,529 km) per hour. This flight set a world speed record for a jet aircraft. Joersz's SR-71A Blackbird took off from a runway and landed on a runway.

Rocket planes have flown much faster. For example, on October 3, 1967, test pilot Pete Knight flew an X-15 rocket plane 4,520 miles (7,274 km) per hour. The X-15 did not take off from a runway. Instead it was launched from a B-52 aircraft. The B-52 was flying at about 500 miles (805 km) per hour at a height of 45,000 feet (13,716 m).

CHAPTER 4

TESTING CIVILIAN AIRCRAFT

The Navy and Air Force teach top pilots how to test hot **military** planes. But pilots are also needed to test many other types of aircraft.

The United States has more than 220,000 **civilian** aircraft of all types. Large passenger jets ferry people between major cities. Small air taxis fly wherever people need them to go. Delivery services like UPS and FedEx have huge fleets of planes. Helicopters speed sick and injured people to hospitals. They also help the police catch crooks.

Each year, designers come up with better plans for aircraft. Cockpit designs change. Computer systems improve. New safety features are added. Stronger and lighter materials are used. Each time a design change is made, someone needs to test it.

Civilian Test Pilot Training

Where do civilian test pilots get their training? Some attend military schools. Others train in a civilian program like the National Test Pilot School (NTPS).

Before this Swiss helicopter could carry out its rescue missions, a test pilot had to make sure the design was safe to fly.

Many NTPS staff members studied at the Air Force Test Pilot School.

Like the Air Force, NTPS requires a college degree in math, science, or engineering. You need many hours of flying experience before the NTPS will accept you. NTPS graduates may seek jobs testing planes at aircraft companies. Foreign students sometimes become test pilots in their home countries' armed forces.

Going Private

Some famous military test pilots have also flown for private firms. Chuck Yeager is one of them. He retired from the Air Force in 1975. But he didn't stop flying. He set new records putting a Piper plane through its paces. His friend Jackie Cochran also flew for private firms. She tested aircraft in the 1960s for Northrop and Lockheed.

Even for a world-class test pilot, flying a small private plane has its risks. Scott Crossfield was a fighter pilot in the Navy during World War II.   On

Mastering the complex cockpit of a KC-135 Stratotanker requires top-flight piloting skills.

November 20, 1953, he became the first person ever to fly at twice the speed of sound. He set his record in a rocket plane — the Douglas D-558-II Skyrocket. Later he helped design another rocket plane — the X-15.

Crossfield flew the X-15 more than a dozen times. He had some close calls but survived them all. His luck finally ran out in Georgia on April 19, 2006. He wasn't flying a rocket plane that night, or even a jet. He was in the cockpit of his single-engine Cessna 210. A violent storm probably caused the aircraft to go down. Crossfield's body was found at the crash site the next day.

Flying by Computer

"If you want to be a test pilot these days, you need to be more than just good at flying," says Dana Purifoy, a test pilot for NASA. "Many of the upcoming test pilots have several degrees in engineering and computer science."

Today, computers are involved at every stage of aircraft design and testing. On many new planes, computers even control the flight. At critical moments like takeoff and landing, the pilot has an important role to play. Once the plane is in the air, however, computers do most of the work. Before they ever leave the ground, pilots log long hours on computer simulators. Many pilots got their first "flying" experience working the joystick on a home computer.

CHAPTER 5

FRONTIERS OF FLIGHT

lying has come a long way since the early 1900s. The first planes were made of wood, metal, and cloth. They carried one or two passengers and could barely get off the ground.

Boeing says its new 787 Dreamliner is designed to provide more comfort and use less fuel than other passenger jets of similar size.

Today, the Boeing Company is building and testing its newest passenger jet — the 787 Dreamliner. The 787 is made of space-age materials. It can seat more than 250 passengers and crew. It uses 20 percent less fuel than any other plane its size. The aircraft is 206 feet (63 m) long. That's longer than the Wright Brothers' first flight in 1903!

Airplanes and the Environment

Airplanes use a tremendous amount of fuel. This fuel comes from oil. The more oil we use now, the less we have for the future.

Another problem with airplanes is the gases they produce. These gases cause changes in Earth's climate. They are making our world warmer. Scientists believe **global warming** will make the oceans rise. This may cause floods and other disasters.

Aircraft designers hope to create new planes that use less fuel. They would be cheaper to operate. They would use less of the world's oil. And they would help stop global warming. Making sure these new designs are stable and safe will be an important job for future test pilots.

Planes Without Pilots?

Something remarkable happened on November 16, 2004. An X-43A Scramjet screamed across the sky at nearly ten times the speed of sound. The X-43A flew at a height of more than 20 miles (32 km) above Earth's surface. A B-52B launch plane and a **booster rocket** helped it gain speed and altitude. At the end of its brief flight, the X-43A plunged into the ocean.

One thing the aircraft didn't have was a pilot. Pilotless planes have some clear benefits. They can fly at the most extreme speeds and heights. They are perfect for dangerous missions. They can stay aloft for very long times. When they crash, no lives are lost. The U.S. military already makes use of pilotless planes, or **drones.** Pilots on the ground control some of these drones. Others fly mostly on their own.

Pilotless planes are the wave of the future. But pilots — and test pilots — will still be needed for many years to come. Testing a plane is a very complex job. "There are too many factors . . . that a human pilot must test out," says Navy pilot Bill Reuter. "Test piloting is not a profession that is going to disappear."

Launched from midair, NASA's pilotless X-43A has set world speed records for a jet-powered aircraft.

GLOSSARY

aircraft carrier — warships with a deck that an aircraft can take off from and land on

altitude — height above Earth's surface

astronauts — people who are specially trained for spaceflight, as in the U.S. space program

booster rocket — a rocket that pushes a plane or spacecraft to the speed and altitude it needs

cargo — goods carried on a plane, a ship, a train, or another vehicle

civilian — not part of the armed forces

cockpit — the space on an aircraft from which the pilot controls the plane

computer simulator — a computer-controlled model that looks and feels like the real thing

drones — pilotless planes

global warming — the gradual rise in Earth's average temperature

military — related to the armed forces

sonic boom — the loud noise produced when an aircraft reaches supersonic speed

supersonic — faster than the speed of sound

World War II — world conflict fought between 1939 and 1945; the Allies (including the United States, Great Britain, and the Soviet Union) defeated the Axis powers (including Germany and Japan)

TO FIND OUT MORE

Books

Amelia Earhart. Trailblazers of the Modern World (series). Lucia Raatma (World Almanac Library)

Extreme Aircaft! Q & A. Smithsonian Q & A (series). Sarah L. Thomson (HarperCollins Children's Books)

Fantastic Flights: One Hundred Years of Flying on the Edge. Patrick O'Brien (Walker Books for Young Readers)

Flight. Ian Graham (Kingfisher)

Wings and Rockets: The Story of Women in Air and Space. Jeannine Atkins (Farrar, Straus and Giroux)

Web Sites

Edwards Air Force Base
www.edwards.af.mil
This site includes information on the U.S. Air Force Test Pilot School.

NASA — Kids Home
www.nasa.gov/audience/forkids/home/index.html
The official National Aeronautics and Space Administration site focuses on the U.S. space program.

U.S. Naval Test Pilot School
www.usntps.navy.mil/gallery.htm
Look at photos of airplanes and flight simulation classrooms.

INDEX

About the Author

Geoffrey M. Horn has written more than three dozen books for young people and adults, along with hundreds of articles for encyclopedias and other works. He lives in southwestern Virginia, in the foothills of the Blue Ridge Mountains, with his wife, their collie, and six cats. He dedicates this book to Bruce Davidson and Marsha Goldstein and their family.